PARENTING YOUR TWELFTH GRADER

A GUIDE TO MAKING THE MOST OF THE "WHAT'S NEXT?" PHASE

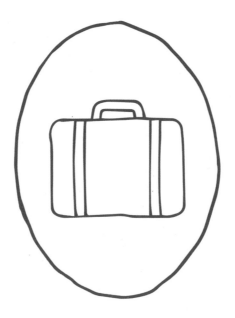

KRISTEN IVY AND REGGIE JOINER

PARENTING YOUR TWELFTH GRADER
A GUIDE TO MAKING THE MOST OF THE
"WHAT'S NEXT?" PHASE

Published by Orange, a division of The reThink Group, Inc.,
5870 Charlotte Lane, Suite 300,
Cumming, GA 30040 U.S.A.

All Scripture quotations, unless otherwise indicated, are taken from the Holy
Bible, New International Version®, NIV®. Copyright ©1973, 1978, 1984, 2011 by
Biblica, Inc.™ Used by permission of Zondervan. All rights reserved worldwide.
www.zondervan.com The "NIV" and "New International Version" are trademarks
registered in the United States Patent and Trademark Office by Biblica, Inc.™

©2017 Kristen Ivy and Reggie Joiner
Authors: Kristen Ivy and Reggie Joiner
Lead Editor: Karen Wilson
Editing Team: Melanie Williams, Hannah Crosby, Sherry Surratt

Art Direction: Ryan Boon and Hannah Crosby
Book Design: FiveStone and Sharon van Rossum

Printed in the United States of America
First Edition 2017
1 2 3 4 5 6 7 8 9 10

"It's hard to connect with your child without first understanding where they are. As counselors and speakers at parenting events across the country, we spend a great deal of time teaching parents about development. To know *where* your child is—not just physically, but emotionally, socially, and spiritually, helps you to truly know and understand *who* your child is. And that understanding is the key to connecting. The Phase Guides give you the tools to do just that. Our wise friends Reggie and Kristen have put together an insightful, hopeful, practical, and literal year-by-year guide that will help you to understand and connect with your child at every age."

SISSY GOFF
M.ED., LPC-MHSP, DIRECTOR OF CHILD & ADOLESCENT COUNSELING AT DAYSTAR COUNSELING MINISTRIES IN NASHVILLE, TENNESSEE, SPEAKER AND AUTHOR OF ARE MY KIDS ON TRACK?

"These resources for parents are fantastically empowering, absolute in their simplicity, and completely doable in every way. The hard work that has gone into the Phase Project will echo through the next generation of children in powerful ways."

JENNIFER WALKER
RN BSN, AUTHOR AND FOUNDER OF MOMS ON CALL

"We all know where we want to end up in our parenting, but how to get there can seem like an unsolved mystery. Through the Phase Project series, Reggie Joiner and Kristen Ivy team up to help us out. The result is a resource that guides us through the different seasons of raising children, and provides a road map to parenting in such a way that we finish up with very few regrets."

SANDRA STANLEY
FOSTER CARE ADVOCATE, BLOGGER, WIFE TO ANDY STANLEY, MOTHER OF THREE

"Not only are the Phase Guides the most creative and well-thought-out guides to parenting I have ever encountered, these books are ESSENTIAL to my daily parenting. With a 13-year-old, 11-year-old, and 9-year-old at home, I am swimming in their wake of daily drama and delicacy. These books are a reminder to enjoy every second. Because it's just a phase."

CARLOS WHITTAKER
AUTHOR, SPEAKER, FATHER OF THREE

"As the founder of Minnie's Food Pantry, I see thousands of people each month with children who will benefit from the advice, guidance, and nuggets of information on how to celebrate and understand the phases of their child's life. Too often we feel like we're losing our mind when sweet little Johnny starts to change his behavior into a person we do not know. I can't wait to start implementing the principles of these books with my clients to remind them . . . it's just a phase."

CHERYL JACKSON
FOUNDER OF MINNIE'S FOOD PANTRY, AWARD-WINNING PHILANTHROPIST, AND GRANDMOTHER

"I began exploring this resource with my counselor hat on, thinking how valuable this will be for the many parents I spend time with in my office. I ended up taking my counselor hat off and putting on my parent hat. Then I kept thinking about friends who are teachers, coaches, youth pastors, and children's ministers, who would want this in their hands. What a valuable resource the Orange team has given us to better understand and care for the kids and adolescents we love. I look forward to sharing it broadly."

DAVID THOMAS
LMSW, DIRECTOR OF FAMILY COUNSELING, DAYSTAR COUNSELING MINISTRIES, SPEAKER AND AUTHOR OF ARE MY KIDS ON TRACK? AND WILD THINGS: THE ART OF NURTURING BOYS

"I have always wished someone would hand me a manual for parenting. Well, the Phase Guides are more than what I wished for. They guide, inspire, and challenge me as a parent—while giving me incredible insight into my children at each age and phase. Our family will be using these every year!"

COURTNEY DEFEO
AUTHOR OF IN THIS HOUSE, WE WILL GIGGLE, MOTHER OF TWO

"As I speak to high school students and their parents, I always wonder to myself: What would it have been like if they had better seen what was coming next? What if they had a guide that would tell them what to expect and how to be ready? What if they could anticipate what is predictable about the high school years before they actually hit? These Phase Guides give a parent that kind of preparation so they can have a plan when they need it most."

JOSH SHIPP
AUTHOR, TEEN EXPERT, AND YOUTH SPEAKER

"The Phase Guides are incredibly creative, well researched, and filled with inspirational actions for everyday life. Each age-specific guide is catalytic for equipping parents to lead and love their kids as they grow up. I'm blown away and deeply encouraged by the content and by its creators. I highly recommend Phase resources for all parents, teachers, and influencers of children. This is the stuff that challenges us and changes our world. Get them. Read them. And use them!"

DANIELLE STRICKLAND
OFFICER WITH THE SALVATION ARMY, AUTHOR, SPEAKER, MOTHER OF TWO

"It's true that parenting is one of life's greatest joys but it is not without its challenges. If we're honest, parenting can sometimes feel like trying to choreograph a dance to an ever-changing beat. It can be clumsy and riddled with well-meaning missteps. If parenting is a dance, this Parenting Guide is a skilled instructor refining your technique and helping you move gracefully to a steady beat. For those of us who love to plan ahead, this guide will help you anticipate what's to come so you can be poised and ready to embrace the moments you want to enjoy."

TINA NAIDOO
MSSW, LCSW EXECUTIVE DIRECTOR, THE POTTER'S HOUSE OF DALLAS, INC.

Special thanks to:

Jim Burns, Ph.D for guidance and consultation on having conversations about sexual integrity

Jon Acuff for guidance and consultation on having conversations about technological responsibility

Jean Sumner, MD for guidance and consultation on having conversations about healthy habits

Every educator, counselor, community leader, and researcher who invested in the Phase Project

TABLE OF CONTENTS

PARENTING YOUR TWELFTH GRADER

HOW TO USE THIS ~~BOOK~~ ~~JOURNAL~~ GUIDE

The guide you hold in your hand doesn't have very many words, but it does have a lot of ideas. Some of these ideas come from thousands of hours of research. Others come from parents, educators, and volunteers who spend every day with kids the same age as yours. This guide won't tell you everything about your kid, but it will tell you a few things about kids at this age.

The best way to use this guide is to take what these pages tell you about twelfth graders and combine it with what you know is true about *your* twelfth grader.

Let's sum it up:

THINGS ABOUT TWELFTH GRADERS +
THOUGHTS ABOUT *YOUR* TWELFTH GRADER =
YOUR GUIDE TO THE NEXT 52 WEEKS OF PARENTING

After each idea in this guide, there are pages with a few questions designed to prompt you to think about your kid, your family, and yourself as a parent. The only guarantee we give to parents who use this guide is this: You will mess up some things as a parent this year. Actually, that's a guarantee to every parent, regardless. But you, you picked up this book! You want to be a better parent. And that's what we hope this guide will do: help you parent your twelfth grader just a little better, simply because you paused to consider a few ideas that can help you make the most of this phase.

THE TWELFTH GRADE PHASE

Remember your senior pictures? Maybe you have one or two stashed away where no one is likely to discover them. But, if you dared look, you're certain they would serve as vivid reminders of your final year of high school, a year full of fear and excitement as you ventured into adulthood and hoped for a bright future.

As I think about my senior picture (in which I was seated on the ugliest '80s velour green chair you can imagine), I quickly relive the roller coaster ride of twelfth grade. Most days I—along with most every other senior—felt like we ruled the high school. But there were also the days when I fearfully raced to my mailbox to see if I had received responses to my college applications. Would there be a thin envelope (never a good thing)? Or a thick envelope (always a good thing)? Often on Friday and Saturday nights, my friends and I had long, wandering conversations as we dreamed about our futures. But then I'd come home and wonder whether I'd accomplish any of those dreams.

As a high school senior, I had one foot firmly planted at home and one foot tentatively stretching for the new terrain awaiting me after graduation. What I needed from my parents—and what your child needs from you—was their willingness and ability to stand close to me in that "in-between" space.

One of the greatest gifts you can offer your senior is an anchor to keep them secure in the unknown waters that lie ahead. Their next steps will be filled with a degree of unpredictability. Whether it's college, military service, or the workforce, the weather can shift from gentle swells to a full-blown tsunami overnight. Twelfth graders need your presence to ground them in a relationship that's steady and predictable.

But there's also a second valuable gift you can offer your senior: Sails that will enable them to explore new waters. There's an adage that states, "A ship in harbor is safe, but that is not what ships are built for." I think that saying perfectly depicts the life of a high school senior. There will be brisk and unfamiliar winds in life after high school. So now, more than every before, they need your help to unfurl their sails and your guidance to discover their vocation and the relationships that God intends for them.

As you parent through this final year of high school, both you and your senior will likely feel stretched. Stretched between the old and the new. Between familiarity and uncertainty. Between "what has been" and "what is to come." That's normal.

But as you launch your senior into the open seas (and into their full potential) remember this: Anchors without sails will leave them hopelessly stuck. Sails without anchors may push them to wander aimlessly. But the two together will set your senior up for the adventure of a lifetime.

- KARA POWELL
EXECUTIVE DIRECTOR OF THE FULLER YOUTH INSTITUTE, AUTHOR, COMMUNICATOR, & MOTHER

52
WEEKS
—
TO PARENT YOUR
TWELFTH GRADER

WHEN YOU SEE
HOW MUCH

Time

YOU HAVE LEFT

—

YOU TEND TO DO

More

WITH THE TIME
YOU HAVE NOW.

THERE ARE APPROXIMATELY

936 WEEKS

FROM THE TIME A BABY IS BORN
UNTIL THEY GROW UP AND MOVE TO
WHATEVER IS NEXT.

You don't have to be much of a mathematician to figure out that at the beginning of your kid's senior year, you only have 52 weeks remaining. This is the final stretch, the bottom of the ninth, the across-the-court buzzer-beater shot. The good news is you're not a rookie parent anymore. You've got this. Stay focused. Make every week count.

Of course, each week might not feel significant. There may be weeks this year when you aren't sure if you had a single conversation with your senior—*where have they been all week?*

Take a deep breath.
You don't have to get everything done this week.

But what happens in your teenager's life week after week, all year, adds up. So, it might be a good idea to create a countdown clock for the last 52 weeks.

CREATE A VISUAL COUNTDOWN.

 Find a jar and fill it with one marble for each week you have remaining with your senior. Then make a habit of removing one marble every week as a reminder to make the most of your time. Make a list. What are a few things you want your senior to experience before this year ends? What do you want to make sure you experience together in this phase?

_____

_____

_____

_____

_____

_____

_____

_____

_____

_____

_____

_____

_____

Where can you place your visual countdown so you will see it frequently?

_____

_____

Which day of the week is best for you to remove a marble?

_____

Is there anything you want to do each week as you remove a marble? (Examples: say a prayer, send an encouraging text, retell a favorite memory)

_____

_____

_____

_____

_____

_____

_____

⚑ At some point, pull out your calendar and go ahead and schedule some of the things you listed above.

EVERY PHASE IS A

TIMEFRAME

IN A KID'S LIFE

WHEN YOU CAN

LEVERAGE

DISTINCTIVE

OPPORTUNITIES

TO INFLUENCE

THEIR

future.

YOU ONLY HAVE
52 WEEKS
WITH YOUR TWELFTH GRADER

while they are still in twelfth grade.
Then they will graduate,
and you will never know them as an twelfth grader again.

Or, to say it another way:
In a few years, your kid will . . .
get a job with health insurance.
pay their own utility bills.
not live in your house (or maybe move back in).

Whether that makes you a little depressed, excited to plan a teenager-free vacation, or maybe a little of both, there's still a lot of opportunity in these next 52 weeks. So, as you count down the weeks with your senior, pay attention to what makes these weeks uniquely different from the weeks you've already spent together and the weeks ahead when they move to the next phase.

Pause to imagine. What might you feel like if you were a senior this year? What might you care about most?

_____

_____

_____

_____

_____

_____

_____

_____

_____

_____

_____

_____

_____

_____

_____

_____

_____

_____

As the parent of a senior, you probably have a different list.
What do you want to appreciate and savor this year?

_____

_____

_____

_____

_____

_____

_____

What are some things you may need to let go of?

_____

_____

_____

_____

_____

_____

_____

_____

What are some things you have noticed about your twelfth grader in this phase that you really enjoy?

_____

_____

_____

_____

_____

_____

_____

_____

_____

_____

_____

_____

_____

_____

_____

_____

_____

_____

What is something new you're learning as a parent during this phase?

_____

_____

_____

_____

_____

_____

_____

_____

_____

_____

_____

_____

_____

_____

_____

_____

_____

_____

_____

_____

_____

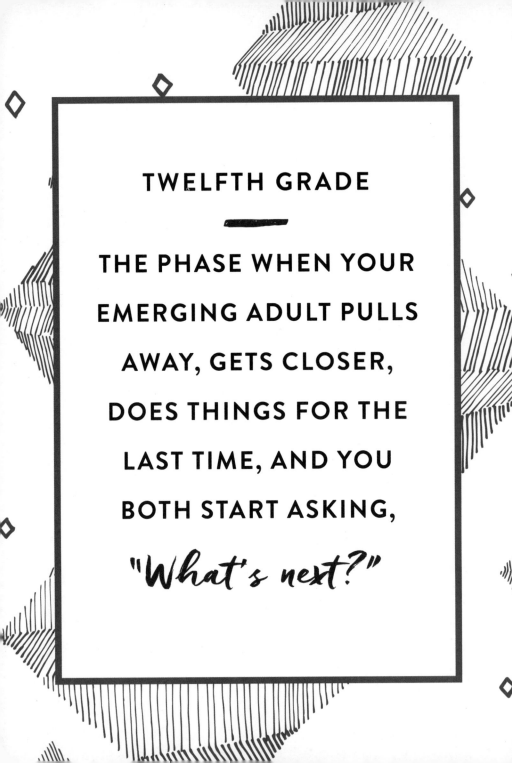

TWELFTH GRADE

—

THE PHASE WHEN YOUR EMERGING ADULT PULLS AWAY, GETS CLOSER, DOES THINGS FOR THE LAST TIME, AND YOU BOTH START ASKING,

"What's next?"

IF SIXTEEN IS "SWEET," EIGHTEEN IS "LEGAL."

Your kid is no longer a kid. Technically speaking, they are responsible for themselves. (Of course, you may still have to pick up the pieces from time to time.) You will feel them pull away as they drive to a first job, deposit a paycheck, or register to vote.

THE COUNTDOWN CLOCK IS RUNNING FAST.

You will probably feel urgency in these last 52 weeks. As a senior takes on more responsibility, they may also lean in relationally. They discover—especially late in the year— they need you a little bit more than they thought. All of a sudden, the decisions they face have very high stakes, like, "Will I date long-distance?"

EVERYONE IS WONDERING, "WHAT'S NEXT?"

In fact, it can drive you both a little crazy. Your senior may mentally check-out of high school long before they feel certain about what they want to do with their future. Even the most accomplished seniors will take a few years (and maybe some counseling) to figure this adult thing out. For now, just remember to focus on the next few months more than the next "rest-of-your-life."

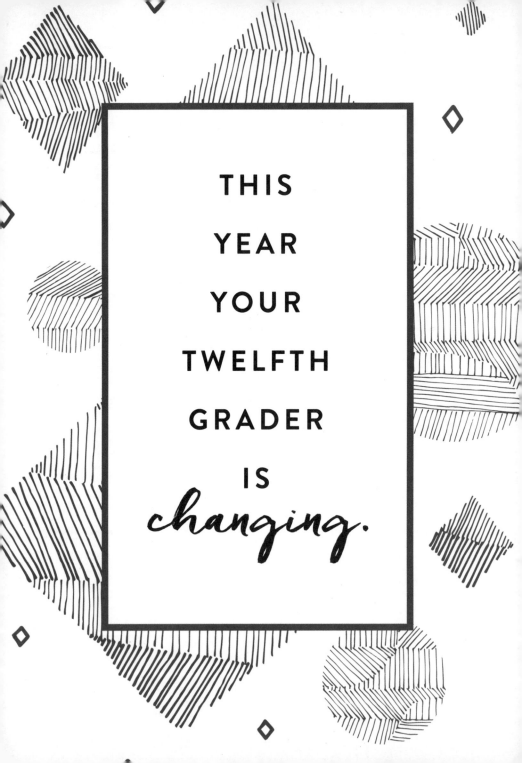

THIS

YEAR

YOUR

TWELFTH

GRADER

IS

changing.

PHYSICALLY

- Wisdom teeth may begin to "come in" (17-21 years)

- Has difficulty falling asleep before 11pm (it's biological)

- Needs nine hours of sleep and one hour of exercise per day

- Girls have likely reached adult height and body development

- Guys may continue to grow in height, and develop muscle mass, body and facial hair

SOCIALLY

- Increased interest in sexual expression (64% of twelfth graders report being sexually active)

- Less available for family time

- Wants to feel ownership in personal decisions

- Shows respect for others' opinions and able to compromise

- More at ease around adults

MENTALLY

- May overly romanticize or catastrophize

- Open to discussing current affairs and social issues

- Capable of complex, multi-step problem solving

- Still struggles with long-term planning

EMOTIONALLY

- Becoming more emotionally stable, but still needs support and grace

- Often thrives in a particular area of interest

- Values being true to themselves

- Frequently demonstrates initiative for personal interests

What are some changes you are noticing in your twelfth grader?

_____

_____

_____

_____

_____

_____

_____

You may disagree with some of the characteristics we've shared about seniors. That's because every twelfth grader is unique. What makes your twelfth grader different from twelfth graders in general?

_____

_____

_____

_____

_____

_____

_____

_____

What are some things that impress you about your senior?

Mark this page. When you start to stress about their un-defined future, pause to consider some of the impressive things you have seen them do. Write them down here. If you want to be really thorough, there are about 52 blank lines.

_____

_____

_____

_____

_____

_____

_____

_____

_____

_____

_____

_____

_____

_____

_____

_____

_____

_____

SIX THINGS

—

EVERY KID
NEEDS

YOUR KID NEEDS **6** THINGS OVER TIME

LOVE

STORIES

WORDS

WORK

PEOPLE

FUN

OVER THE NEXT 52 WEEKS, YOUR TWELFTH GRADER WILL NEED MANY THINGS:

Your senior may be a very different person than they were two years ago, five years ago, or fourteen years ago—when they were coloring scribble pictures for you to display on the refrigerator. Many of their needs have changed. But there are still six things your senior needs just as much as they always have.

EVERY KID, AT EVERY PHASE, NEEDS . . .

LOVE
to give them a
sense of WORTH.

STORIES
to give them a bigger
PERSPECTIVE.

WORK
to give them
PURPOSE.

FUN
to give them
CONNECTION.

PEOPLE
to give them
BELONGING.

WORDS
to give them
DIRECTION.

The next few pages are designed to help you think about how you will give your teenager these six things, right now, while they are a senior.

ONE QUESTION YOUR TWELFTH GRADER IS ASKING

Graduation is a crisis—for both of you. Sure, it's exciting. It's a huge accomplishment. But something is about to change, and there's a good chance you aren't convinced they're ready. They might not be. And whether they seem to show it or not, your senior is probably just as concerned about that as you.

Your twelfth grader is asking one major question:

"WHAT WILL I DO?"

It's easy for senior year to become a negative feedback loop where your concern for their future escalates either their rebellion or their stress, or both. So relax. No senior is ready for the rest of their life. Your senior just needs for you to love them and to do one thing:

MOBILIZE their potential.

Help them prepare as best as possible for what's coming next. When you mobilize your senior's potential you communicate . . .

"I love you today,"

"We can handle tomorrow,"

and "Let's think together about your best next step."

As you consider how to mobilize your senior's potential, there may be tension between right now, next year, and the rest of their life. Start with the end. What are the most important things you want to be true for their future?

_____

_____

_____

_____

_____

_____

_____

_____

_____

_____

_____

_____

_____

_____

_____

_____

_____

What might be some things your senior could do this year that would help those things become reality?

_____

_____

_____

_____

_____

_____

_____

_____

_____

_____

_____

_____

_____

_____

_____

_____

_____

_____

_____

What is most important to your senior, right now? How can you continue to support their interests?

_____

_____

_____

_____

_____

_____

_____

_____

_____

_____

_____

_____

_____

_____

_____

_____

_____

_____

_____

_____

What are some things that matter most this year when it comes to engaging their interests, enjoying senior year, and preparing for future next steps?

_____

_____

_____

_____

_____

_____

_____

_____

_____

_____

_____

_____

_____

_____

_____

_____

_____

_____

EVERY KID

NEEDS

stories

OVER TIME

—

TO GIVE THEM

A BIGGER

perspective.

BOOKS YOUR TWELFTH GRADER MIGHT BE READING

THINGS FALL APART
by Chinua Achebe

DO OVER
by Jon Acuff

HOW TO WIN FRIENDS & INFLUENCE PEOPLE
by Dale Carnegie

QUIET: THE POWER OF INTROVERTS IN A WORLD THAT CAN'T STOP TALKING
by Susan Cain

THE ALCHEMIST
by Paulo Coelho

THE RED TENT
by Anita Diamant

PILLARS OF THE EARTH (SERIES)
by Ken Follett

OUTLIERS
by Malcolm Gladwell

LOVE DOES
by Bob Goff

A TIME TO KILL
by John Grisham

A MILLION MILES IN A THOUSAND YEARS
by Donald Miller

SAME KIND OF DIFFERENT AS ME
by Ron Hall and Denver Moore

SIDDHARTHA
by Herman Hesse

THE GREAT DIVORCE
by C.S. Lewis

ANGELA'S ASHES
by Frank McCourt

ATONEMENT
by Ian McEwan

THE BLUEST EYE
by Toni Morrison

THREE CUPS OF TEA
by Greg Mortenson and David Oliver Relin

READING LOLITA IN TEHRAN
by Azar Nafisi

THE BELL JAR
by Sylvia Plath

Share a story. Whether it's a book, play, TV series, or movie, what are some stories that engage your twelfth grader? What might happen to your relationship when you watch or read the same story together?

_____

_____

_____

_____

_____

_____

_____

_____

_____

_____

_____

_____

_____

_____

_____

_____

_____

_____

Live a story. When a twelfth grader serves others, they broaden their perspective by learning about someone else's story. Is there somewhere your senior would enjoy serving others on a regular basis?

_____

_____

_____

_____

_____

_____

_____

_____

_____

_____

_____

_____

_____

_____

_____

_____

_____

THE END OF THIS YEAR WILL BE THE BEGINNING OF A NEW ADVENTURE.

Help your teenager prepare for what's ahead by remembering how far they have come.

How have you seen your senior overcome challenges?

_____

_____

_____

_____

_____

_____

_____

_____

_____

_____

_____

_____

_____

_____

How have you seen them develop a unique skill or ability?

_____

_____

_____

_____

_____

_____

_____

_____

_____

_____

_____

_____

_____

_____

_____

_____

_____

_____

_____

_____

_____

_____

WORK YOUR TWELFTH GRADER CAN DO

DO HOMEWORK

MANAGE A PERSONAL CALENDAR

PREPARE A MEAL PLAN, GROCERY LIST, AND HELP COOK FAMILY MEALS

SORT, WASH, FOLD, AND PUT AWAY LAUNDRY

RUN FAMILY ERRANDS
("Can you grab some milk at the store before you come home?")

MAKE APPOINTMENTS
(doctor, hair cut, dentist, etc.)

GET A PART-TIME JOB OR INTERNSHIP

MANAGE A BUDGET

HELP PAY PERSONAL BILLS
(insurance, phone bill, etc.)

REGISTER TO VOTE
(when they turn 18)

SOLIDIFY A POST-HIGH SCHOOL PLAN

REFINE A SKILL: ART, MUSICAL, TECHNICAL, MECHANICAL, OR ATHLETIC

What are some ways your senior already shows responsibility at home, at school, and in-between?

_____

_____

_____

_____

_____

_____

_____

_____

_____

_____

_____

_____

_____

_____

_____

_____

_____

_____

How can you collaborate with your senior to agree on which of their responsibilities matter most for your family and their future?

_____

_____

_____

_____

_____

_____

_____

_____

_____

_____

_____

_____

_____

_____

_____

_____

_____

_____

_____

Some days might be easier than others to motivate your senior. What are some strategies you could employ to keep your senior motivated? *(This may be hardest after January.)*

_____

_____

_____

_____

_____

_____

_____

_____

_____

_____

_____

_____

_____

_____

_____

_____

_____

What are things your senior will need to be able to do independently next year? How are you helping them develop those skills now?

_____

_____

_____

_____

_____

_____

_____

_____

_____

_____

_____

_____

_____

_____

_____

_____

EVERY KID

NEEDS

fun

OVER TIME

—

TO GIVE

THEM

connection.

WAYS TO HAVE FUN
WITH YOUR TWELFTH GRADER

WATCH A MOVIE

ATTEND A SPORTING EVENT

GO TO A CONCERT

WORK OUT TOGETHER

PLAY MUSIC TOGETHER

BUILD SOMETHING

COOK SOMETHING

GO ON A RUN

GO ON A HIKE

GO SHOPPING

SHOOT SOME HOOPS

WORK ON CAR REPAIRS

GET A MANICURE

WATCH A T.V. SERIES

GO TO A PLAY

GO FISHING

GO BOWLING

PLAY LASER TAG

HAVE A RESTAURANT THAT'S "YOURS"

TRY A NEW RESTAURANT OR FOOD TRUCK

PLANT A GARDEN

PLAY A BOARD GAME

PLAY A VIDEO GAME

PLAY CARDS

PLAY A GAME ON A PHONE APP

LAUNCH MODEL ROCKETS

LEARN TO DANCE

GO TO THE LAKE

RIDE A ROLLER COASTER

GO OUT FOR COFFEE

GO OUT FOR ICE CREAM

GO SEE A COMEDIAN

Whatever you do together for fun, try to offer suggestions based on what they enjoy—even at the expense of what you might enjoy a little more.

What are some of the activities you and your twelfth grader have enjoyed in the past? *(Think about which of these you can continue to do this year and in the years ahead.)*

_____

_____

_____

_____

_____

_____

_____

_____

_____

_____

_____

_____

_____

_____

_____

_____

_____

What are some new things you might want to do for fun with your twelfth grader this year?

_____

_____

_____

_____

_____

_____

_____

When are the best times of the day, or week, for you to set aside to just have fun with your twelfth grader?

_____

_____

_____

_____

_____

_____

_____

Some days are *extra* fun days. What are some ways you want to celebrate the special days coming up this year?

NEXT BIRTHDAY

_____

_____

_____

_____

_____

_____

_____

_____

_____

_____

_____

_____

_____

_____

_____

_____

HOLIDAYS

_____
_____
_____
_____
_____
_____
_____
_____
_____
_____
_____
_____
_____
_____
_____
_____
_____
_____
_____
_____
_____
_____
_____

GRADUATION

_____

_____

_____

_____

_____

_____

_____

_____

_____

_____

_____

_____

_____

_____

_____

_____

_____

_____

_____

_____

_____

_____

_____

_____
_____
_____
_____
_____
_____
_____
_____
_____
_____
_____
_____
_____
_____
_____
_____
_____
_____
_____
_____
_____
_____

EVERY KID

NEEDS

people

OVER TIME

—

TO GIVE

THEM

belonging.

ADULTS WHO MIGHT INFLUENCE YOUR TWELFTH GRADER

PARENTS

COMMUNITY LEADERS

CHURCH LEADERS

GRANDPARENTS

FRIENDS' PARENTS

COACHES

COLLEGE OR GRADUATE STUDENTS
(really young adults)

HIGH SCHOOL TEACHERS

BOSS OR CO-WORKERS
(at an afterschool job)

As great as you are *(and you're clearly an awesome parent)* you aren't the only adult influence your twelfth grader needs. List at least five adults who have the potential to positively influence your twelfth grader.

_____

_____

_____

_____

_____

_____

_____

_____

_____

_____

_____

_____

_____

_____

_____

_____

_____

_____

What would be good information for these people to know if
they want to help or support your twelfth grader this year?

_____

_____

_____

_____

_____

_____

_____

What are a few ways you could show these adults appreciation
for the significant role they play in your kid's life?

_____

_____

_____

_____

_____

_____

_____

Relationships provide support through transitional times. How can you include these adults in celebrating your senior at the end of the year?

_____

_____

_____

_____

_____

_____

_____

_____

_____

_____

_____

_____

_____

_____

_____

_____

_____

_____

How could you encourage these adults to stay connected with your senior throughout next year?

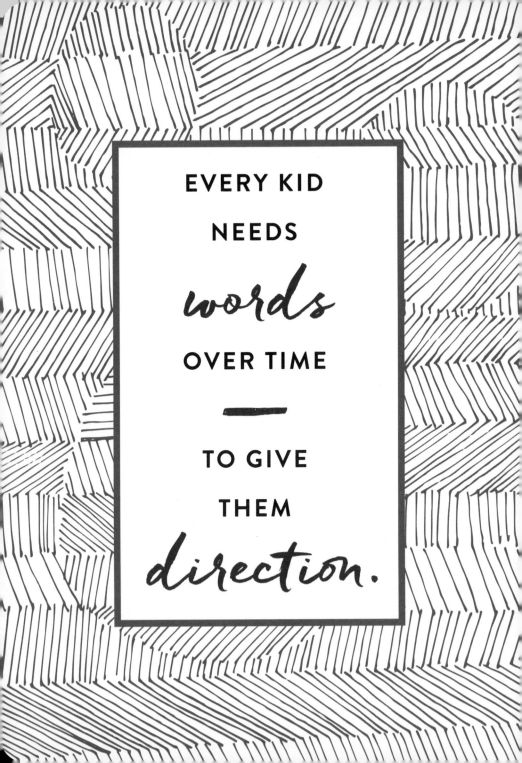

EVERY KID

NEEDS

words

OVER TIME

—

TO GIVE

THEM

direction.

WORDS YOUR TWELFTH GRADER NEEDS TO HEAR

GOOD MORNING!

I LOVE YOU

I'M SORRY THAT I . . .

I BELIEVE IN YOU

WHAT DO YOU THINK?

YOU'RE REALLY BECOMING . . .

WANT A HUG?

I LIKE YOU

ME TOO

TELL ME MORE

I KNOW YOU WILL MAKE GOOD CHOICES NEXT YEAR BECAUSE . . .

I DON'T KNOW, BUT LET'S FIGURE IT OUT

I LIKE HAVING YOU AROUND

GOOD NIGHT!

I'M LISTENING

THAT MUST BE HARD. HOW CAN I HELP?

What are some ways you can share personal and specific encouragement with your twelfth grader?

Hint: You might start with the things that impress you about your twelfth grader from page 29.

As your relationship shifts, so will your language. What are things you say that you've noticed your senior resisting?

Hint: You might ask them, "Do you ever feel like I don't talk to you like an adult? What are some things I should stop saying?"

_____

_____

_____

_____

_____

_____

_____

_____

_____

_____

_____

_____

_____

_____

_____

_____

_____

_____

_____

What do you want to say this year that you hope your senior will remember? *(Consider writing a graduation toast or a letter you can give them as they move on to whatever is next.)*

_____

_____

_____

_____

_____

_____

_____

_____

_____

_____

_____

_____

_____

_____

_____

_____

_____

_____

FOUR CONVERSATIONS
—

TO HAVE IN THIS PHASE

WHEN YOU KNOW
WHERE YOU WANT
TO GO,

AND YOU KNOW
WHERE YOU ARE
NOW,

YOU CAN ALWAYS
DO SOMETHING

TO MOVE IN A
BETTER DIRECTION.

OVER THE NEXT 52 WEEKS, IT MAY BE HARD TO FIND TIME FOR CONVERSATIONS. WHEN YOU *DO* GET A FEW MINUTES TO TALK, IT CAN BE HARD TO KNOW WHAT TO SAY FIRST.

You want to talk about applications (job, college, loan, housing). They want to ask for money to go to prom.

But, in the middle of everything that's urgent, don't forget to have a few important conversations along the way as well.

WHAT YOU SAY ABOUT . . .	MAY IMPACT THEIR FUTURE EVEN MORE THAN THAT PILE OF UNTOUCHED APPLICATIONS ON THEIR NIGHTSTAND.
Health	
Sex	
Technology	
or Faith	

The next pages are about the conversations that matter most. On the left page is a destination—what you might want to be true in your kid's life 52 weeks from now (and into the next chapter). On the right page is a goal for conversations with your twelfth grader this year and a few suggestions about what you might want to say.

Healthy habits

—

LEARNING TO STRENGTHEN MY BODY THROUGH EXERCISE, NUTRITION, AND SELF-ADVOCACY

THIS YEAR YOU WILL

ENCOURAGE A HEALTHY LIFESTYLE

SO THEY WILL SHARPEN THEIR PERSONAL AWARENESS AND BALANCE DIET AND EXERCISE.

Your senior still needs an annual physical, but it may be time to look for a new primary healthcare provider. Talk to your pediatrician and get a recommendation. When the time comes, make sure to get a copy of, and transfer, all medical records. You can also encourage your twelfth grader to develop healthy habits with a few simple words.

SAY THINGS LIKE . . .

"I BOUGHT MORE TRAIL MIX AND THERE'S SOME YOGURT IN THE FRIDGE."
(Stock the kitchen with healthy options.)

"CAN I MAKE YOU SOME EGGS BEFORE YOU HEAD OUT?"
(Encourage breakfast.)

"WHAT DO YOU THINK ARE HEALTHY BOUNDARIES FOR DRINKING?"
(Talk about personal boundaries for future health.)

WOULD YOU LIKE TO GO ON A RUN WITH ME?
(Stay active together.)

"WHEN CAN WE HAVE DINNER TOGETHER THIS WEEK?"
(Eat meals together— whenever possible.)

What are your senior's favorite ways to exercise? How can you help them have access to exercise now and 52 weeks from now?

_____

_____

_____

_____

_____

_____

_____

_____

_____

_____

_____

_____

_____

_____

_____

_____

_____

_____

Do you feel confident about your senior's ability to select and prepare meals? How can you help them access healthy food options both now and 52 weeks from now?

_____

_____

_____

_____

_____

_____

_____

_____

_____

_____

_____

_____

_____

_____

_____

_____

_____

_____

Do you have any specific concerns when it comes to your senior's physical or mental health? Who will help you monitor and improve their health this year and next?

_____

_____

_____

_____

_____

_____

_____

_____

_____

_____

_____

_____

_____

_____

_____

_____

_____

What are your own health goals for this year? How can you improve the habits in your own life?

_____

_____

_____

_____

_____

_____

_____

_____

_____

_____

_____

_____

_____

_____

_____

_____

_____

_____

_____

_____

Sexual integrity

—

GUARDING MY
POTENTIAL FOR
INTIMACY THROUGH
APPROPRIATE
BOUNDARIES
AND MUTUAL
RESPECT

THIS YEAR YOU WILL

COACH THEM TOWARD HEALTHY RELATIONSHIPS

SO THEY WILL ESTABLISH PERSONAL BOUNDARIES AND PRACTICE MUTUAL RESPECT.

The hardest thing about being a coach is that no matter how much you care about the players, you can't control every play of the game. By now, you've probably discovered the same is true about parenting your senior. But like a good coach, you can help your senior refine a few skills that could promote sexual integrity.

SAY THINGS LIKE . . .

DO YOU WANT TO TALK ABOUT IT?

ARE YOU OKAY?

"THANK YOU FOR TALKING ABOUT THIS. CAN WE TALK ABOUT IT AGAIN ANOTHER TIME?"
(Always finish the conversation with room to pick it back up again later.)

"I'M SO GLAD YOU ASKED ME."

"NO BOYFRIENDS ON FAMILY VACATIONS."
(Don't make future break-ups harder.)

"HAVE YOU TALKED ABOUT WHETHER YOU PLAN TO STAY TOGETHER NEXT YEAR?"

"EVEN IF HE TEXTS YOU THAT HE'S HERE, INVITE HIM IN TO SAY HELLO."
(Create opportunities for boyfriends/girlfriends to connect with you.)

"DO YOU WANT TO BE IN A RELATIONSHIP NEXT YEAR?"
(Prompt conversations about their future hopes and plans.)

What are some ways your senior has demonstrated sexual integrity?

_____

_____

_____

_____

_____

_____

_____

_____

_____

_____

_____

_____

_____

_____

_____

_____

_____

_____

_____

What are some weak spots where you are still coaching your senior to strengthen personal boundaries or mutual respect?

Based on what you've watched your senior navigate so far in life, what are some strengths they might bring into their future relationships?

_____

_____

_____

_____

_____

_____

_____

_____

_____

_____

_____

_____

_____

_____

_____

_____

_____

_____

_____

Based on what you know about your kid, and what you've seen in their relationships, what are some qualities you hope they will find in a future spouse?

Technological responsibility

—

LEVERAGING THE
POTENTIAL OF ONLINE
EXPERIENCES TO
ENHANCE MY OFFLINE
COMMUNITY
AND SUCCESS

THIS YEAR YOU WILL

EXPAND THEIR POTENTIAL

SO THEY WILL ESTABLISH PERSONAL BOUNDARIES AND LEVERAGE ONLINE OPPORTUNITIES.

As the clock runs down, and your senior moves further and further away, technology can be a great way to stay connected relationally. Learn how your senior uses technology to connect and leverage those platforms.

SAY THINGS LIKE . . .

> **CAN I PUT YOUR SCHEDULE IN MY CALENDAR SO I KNOW WHAT YOUR WEEK IS LIKE?**

"WHAT'S THE BEST WAY FOR ME TO TALK TO YOU DURING THE DAY?"

"LOOK WHERE I AM TODAY. I'M THINKING ABOUT YOU!"
(Share pictures with each other.)

"I'M SO PROUD OF YOU. WOULD IT BE OKAY IF I POST A PICTURE TO SHARE YOUR ACCOMPLISHMENT?"

"SAW THIS VIDEO AND THOUGHT YOU MIGHT LIKE IT."

"CAN I SEE WHAT YOU'VE BEEN CREATING LATELY?"
(Show interest in everything from art to engineering to design to fan websites.)

What are some ways you've seen your senior use technology to do something good?

_____

_____

_____

_____

_____

_____

_____

_____

_____

_____

_____

_____

_____

_____

_____

_____

_____

_____

_____

What are ways you have seen or heard about other parents leveraging technology to stay connected with their children after graduation?

_____

_____

_____

_____

_____

_____

_____

_____

_____

_____

_____

_____

_____

_____

_____

_____

_____

_____

When you aren't sure what to do about an issue related to parenting and technology, who can you go to for advice?

_____

_____

_____

_____

_____

_____

_____

_____

_____

_____

_____

_____

_____

_____

_____

_____

_____

_____

What are your own personal values and disciplines when it comes to leveraging technology? Are there ways you want to improve your own savvy, skill, or responsibility in this area?

_____

_____

_____

_____

_____

_____

_____

_____

_____

_____

_____

_____

_____

_____

_____

_____

_____

Authentic faith

—

TRUSTING JESUS
IN A WAY THAT
TRANSFORMS HOW
I LOVE GOD,
MYSELF,
AND THE REST
OF THE WORLD

THIS YEAR YOU WILL

FUEL PASSION

**SO THEY WILL KEEP PURSUING AUTHENTIC FAITH
AND DISCOVER A PERSONAL MISSION.**

Your senior may be preparing to transition—not only out of their school and your home, but also potentially out of your church. When you talk with your senior about what's next for them, include conversations about how they will find and serve in a faith community.

SAY THINGS LIKE . . .

WHAT DO YOU LIKE ABOUT CHURCH/ YOUTH GROUP?
(Talk about the value of a faith community.)

"HOW CAN I PRAY FOR YOU TODAY / THIS WEEK?"

"WHEN DO YOU FEEL CLOSE TO GOD?"

"I DON'T KNOW."

"WHAT'S SOMETHING YOU FEEL LIKE GOD IS TEACHING YOU RIGHT NOW?"

"THAT'S A GOOD QUESTION. I'M NOT SURE I WILL EVER KNOW THE FULL ANSWER, BUT I BELIEVE ..."
(Let them know it's okay to talk about hard questions.)

"LATELY, I'M FINDING I CONNECT BEST WITH GOD WHEN I'M ..."

"THERE'S NOTHING YOU WILL EVER DO THAT COULD MAKE GOD STOP LOVING YOU."

"ARE THERE WAYS YOU WOULD WANT TO SERVE IN OUR CHURCH OR COMMUNITY?"

What do you want to be true for your senior's faith this year—and in the years to come?

_____

_____

_____

_____

_____

_____

_____

_____

_____

_____

_____

_____

_____

_____

_____

_____

_____

_____

_____

_____

What are some ways you can help deepen your senior's connection with friends and adult leaders who follow Jesus?

Who has been influential in your kid's faith? How can you encourage them to stay connected with your senior as they transition to what's next?

_____

_____

_____

_____

_____

_____

_____

_____

_____

_____

_____

_____

_____

_____

_____

_____

_____

_____

Once you know where your senior will live next year, how can you help them find a new faith community or redefine the way they connect with their present community?

_____

_____

_____

_____

_____

_____

_____

_____

_____

_____

_____

_____

_____

_____

_____

_____

_____

_____

_____

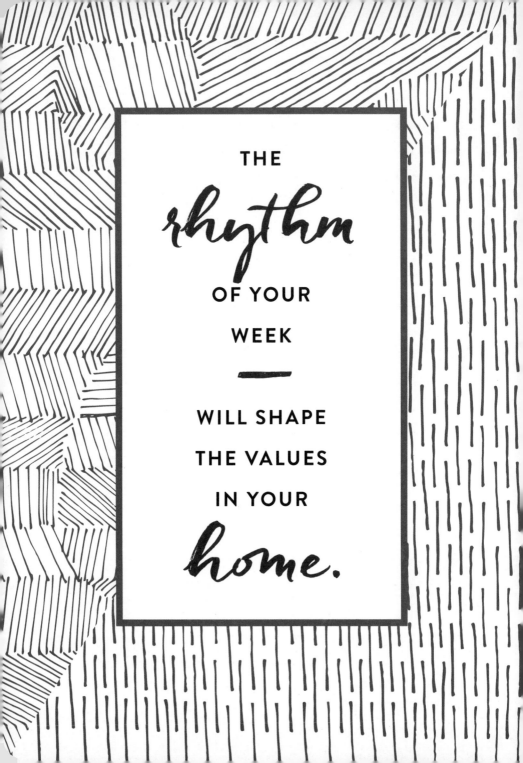

THE

rhythm

OF YOUR

WEEK

—

WILL SHAPE

THE VALUES

IN YOUR

home.

NOW THAT YOU HAVE FILLED THIS BOOK WITH IDEAS, IT MAY SEEM AS IF YOU WILL NEVER HAVE TIME TO GET IT ALL DONE.

Actually, you have *52 weeks until graduation.*

You have opportunities to connect with your senior in ways you might never have in the same way again. So make the most of this phase by spending time together—even if it's only an hour each week. Look for opportunities during three consistent times (and one that's a little less predictable).

Instill purpose by starting the day with encouraging words.

Connect regularly by scheduling time to eat together (even if it's once a week).

Interpret life when they occasionally open up at the end of the day (stay consistently available—just in case).

Strengthen your relationship by adjusting your plans to show up whenever they need you.

Write down any other thoughts or questions you have about parenting your senior now, and in the years to come. Who can you go to for parenting advice as you and your senior transition to what's next?

_____

_____

_____

_____

_____

_____

_____

_____

_____

_____

_____

_____

_____

_____

_____

_____

YOU HAVE

APPROXIMATELY

52 WEEKS.

EVERY KID $\longrightarrow$ MADE IN THE IMAG OF GOD

Incite *wonder* $\longrightarrow$ SO THEY WILL . . .
KNOW GOD'S LOVE
& MEET GOD'S FAMILY

BEGINNING
(Baby dedication)

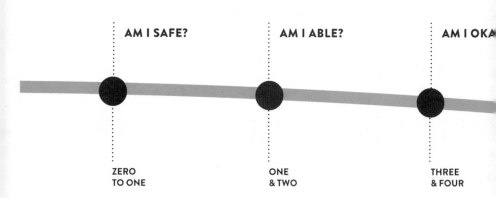

AM I SAFE?	AM I ABLE?	AM I OKA
ZERO TO ONE	ONE & TWO	THREE & FOUR

EMBRACE *their physical needs*

E  **TO** *LOVE GOD*

Provoke
discovery $\longrightarrow$

SO THEY WILL . . .
TRUST GOD'S CHARACTER
& EXPERIENCE GOD'S FAMILY

 WISDOM
(First day of school)

 FAITH
(Trust Jesus)

Y?

DO I HAVE YOUR ATTENTION?

DO I HAVE WHAT IT TAKES?

DO I HAVE FRIENDS?

K & FIRST

SECOND & THIRD

FOURTH & FIFTH

ENGAGE **their interests**

_____
_____
_____
_____
_____
_____
_____
_____
_____
_____
_____
_____
_____
_____
_____
_____
_____
_____
_____
_____
_____
_____
_____
_____
_____

IT'S JUST
A PHASE
SO DON'T
MISS IT.

ND

trust Jesus → TO HAVE A BETTER FUTURE

Fuel

passion →

SO THEY WILL . . .
**KEEP PURSUING AUTHENTIC FAITH
& DISCOVER A PERSONAL MISSION**

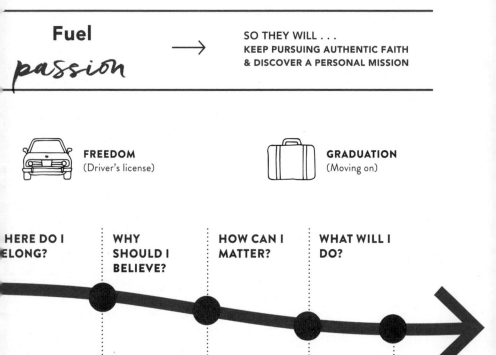

FREEDOM
(Driver's license)

GRADUATION
(Moving on)

| HERE DO I ELONG? | WHY SHOULD I BELIEVE? | HOW CAN I MATTER? | WHAT WILL I DO? |

| TH | TENTH | ELEVENTH | TWELFTH | 18+ |

MOBILIZE their potential

WITH
ALL THEIR

 HEART SOUL STRENGTH

Provoke
discovery →

SO THEY WILL . . .
OWN THEIR OWN FAITH
& VALUE A FAITH COMMUNITY

 IDENTITY
(Coming of age)

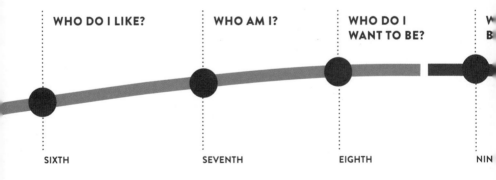

WHO DO I LIKE?

WHO AM I?

**WHO DO I
WANT TO BE?**

W
B

SIXTH

SEVENTH

EIGHTH

NIN

AFFIRM their personal journey

ABOUT THE AUTHORS

KRISTEN IVY @kristen_ivy

Kristen Ivy is executive director of the Phase Project. She and her husband, Matt, are in the preschool and elementary phases with three kids: Sawyer, Hensley, and Raleigh.

Kristen earned her Bachelors of Education from Baylor University in 2004 and received a Master of Divinity from Mercer University in 2009. She worked in the public school system as a high school biology and English teacher, where she learned firsthand the importance of influencing the next generation.

Kristen is also the President at Orange and has played an integral role in the development of the elementary, middle school, and high school curriculum and has shared her experiences at speaking events across the country. She is the co-author of *Playing for Keeps*, *Creating a Lead Small Culture*, *It's Just a Phase*, and *Don't Miss It*.

REGGIE JOINER @reggiejoiner

Reggie Joiner is founder and CEO of the reThink Group and co-founder of the Phase Project. He and his wife, Debbie, have reared four kids into adulthood. They now also have two grandchildren.

The reThink Group (also known as Orange) is a non-profit organization whose purpose is to influence those who influence the next generation. Orange provides resources and training for churches and organizations that create environments for parents, kids, and teenagers.

Before starting the reThink Group in 2006, Reggie was one of the founders of North Point Community Church. During his 11 years with Andy Stanley, Reggie was the executive director of family ministry, where he developed a new concept for relevant ministry to children, teenagers, and married adults. Reggie has authored and co-authored more than 10 books including: *Think Orange, Seven Practices of Effective Ministry, Parenting Beyond Your Capacity, Playing for Keeps, Lead Small, Creating a Lead Small Culture*, and his latest, *A New Kind of Leader* and *Don't Miss It.*

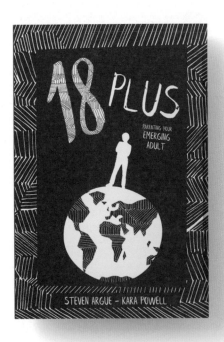

MAKE THE MOST OF EVERY PHASE IN YOUR CHILD'S LIFE

Congratulations! You've parented for 936 weeks, and your kid has graduated and moved on to what's next. Whether they still live at home or you've already converted their room into a workout studio, you might be in the best phase of your kid's life. While parenting won't look the same anymore, it isn't over yet. Your kid still needs you.

Designed in partnership with Parent Cue, each guide will help you rediscover . . .

your emerging adult is changing,
how their world is changing, and
what they still need from you.

 **PARENT CUE**

Be the parent you want to be.

At Parent Cue, our goal is to cue you with what you need, when you need it—curated content, weekly inspiration, free resources, products and more—so you are equipped to be the parent you want to be.

MORE RESOURCES AT   **WWW.PARENTCUE.ORG**